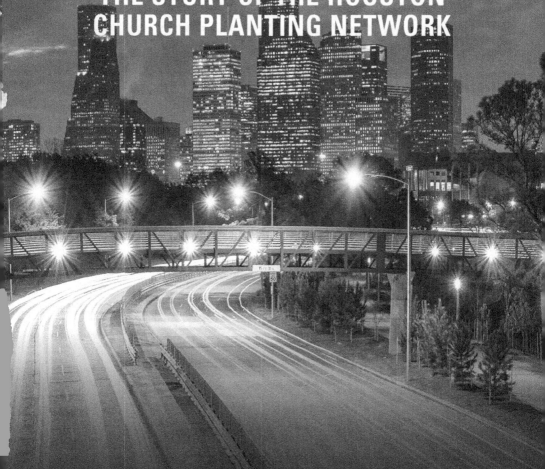

# COLLABORATION
## FOR
# MULTIPLICATION

## THE STORY OF THE HOUSTON
## CHURCH PLANTING NETWORK

*Collaboration for Multiplication: The Story of the Houston*
*Church Planting Network*

Copyright © 2015 by Bruce Wesley
All rights reserved.
ISBN-13: 978-1517569570
ISBN-10: 1517569575

Exponential is a growing movement of leaders committed to the spread of healthy new churches. Exponential Resources spotlights and spreads actionable principles, ideas and solutions for the accelerated multiplication of healthy, reproducing faith communities. For more information, visit exponential.org

This book is manufactured in the United States.

Edited by Lindy Lowry
Cover Design and Layout by Karen Pheasant and Story.GS

# ABOUT THE
# CHURCH UNIQUE INTENTIONAL
# LEADER SERIES

## THE SERIES ORIGINATED UNEXPECTEDLY

Some things are found along the way, not calculated. Twelve years ago, my call into gospel ministry transitioned from pastoring in a local church to providing vision and strategy coaching for many churches. By God's grace I found unusual favor with a wide variety of pastors in different faith tribes and church models. I never planned to write, but eventually a passion for tool making would develop. Why? I observed firsthand how the right tool, at the right time, can change the trajectory of a church leader's calling. And it all started with the book Church Unique.

## THE SERIES IS NOT FOR EVERYONE

Please know that this series is not about minor improvements in your ministry. It's written with a higher aim—changed trajectory. Therefore it carries a bold voice and challenging ideas. It's not written to make you feel good or to entertain. It's not an aggregation of good-idea blog posts. In fact, it's not really written for most church leaders. It's written for the hungry-to-learn leader, the passionate dreamer and the disciplined doer. It's written for the intentional few.

## THE SERIES IS A UNIQUE COLLECTION

I grew up with a dad who worked non-stop around the house. He bought only Craftsman tools. I can remember the trademark red color of the Philips screwdrivers and the signature-shape of the chrome wrenches. The reason he bought Craftsman was the lifetime guarantee. The reason I liked them is they felt different in my hand.

So how will the Intentional Leader Series look and feel different? We aim for these features:

- **High transferability through model-transcendent principles.** We are not creating tools to guide the strategy or tactics of one approach. Most books do this even without explicitly acknowledging it. Every book is applicable to any ministry model.

- **Immediate usability on the front line of ministry.** The tools have been refined in real, messy ministry. We will prioritize the application for your leadership huddle or staff meeting next week.

- **Clarity-first conviction.** This series connects to the foundational work in Church Unique; and each book, while able to stand on its own, will relate to and reference the fundamental tools like the Kingdom Concept and Vision Frame. The books will relate more like engine gears than like distant cousins.

- **To-the-point style.** These aren't gift books or lite e-books created for advertising purposes. We want to bring short reads with sharp insight. We want a tool you can read in an hour, but change your leadership forever.

- **Gospel confidence.** The only real power center for ministry is the Gospel and we are not ashamed of this reality! (Romans 1:16) Therefore, no growth technique or creative innovation or smart idea should diminish a Gospel-centered outlook on ministry. This series will remind the reader that Jesus is sovereignly building His church (Matthew 16:18).

I hope you enjoy the contents of the series as we strive to bring you tools that are transferable, usable, integrated and direct. More than this, I hope they challenge your thinking and make you a better leader in your time and your place. Please stay in touch at WillMancini.com.

Will Mancini

*I was incredibly inspired reading the story of the Houston Church Planters Network. I had the privilege of sitting around a table with these leaders and hearing first hand their passion, unity and collaboration. It's inspiring! I'm jealous for this to happen in Memphis and you will want it to happen in your city as well. Awesome.*

**John Bryson**
Teaching Pastor, Fellowship Memphis

*Jesus never intended the Church to be unified just for unity's sake. Unity is for the sake of mission. Thus, the collaboration that leads to multiplication described in this book is incumbent upon every church and network in every city that desires to saturate their geography with the gospel. With the platform of Exponential and the multiplication mission they embrace, HCPN has added a welcome challenge and resource to every leader in every city who is serious about the gospel being heard and seen by every man, woman, and child.*

**Jerry Gillis**
Lead Pastor, The Chapel, Buffalo, NY

*This is a tale that needs to be told in more cities across our nation. It is inspiring to see churches come together on mission and each sacrificially give to the churching of an entire city like HCPN has done. Bravo. I look forward to reading all the remaining chapters to this story.*

**Neil Cole**
Church planter and Author of many books including: Organic Church, Church 3.0 and Primal Fire

*This book is so helpful. It is concise, informative, readable, honest and real. I was challenged, inspired, provoked and encouraged. It's not a big read so there's no good reason for anyone not reading it.*

**Steve Timmis**
Executive Director, Acts 29 Network | Pastor, The Crowded House, Sheffield, UK

*Over a lifetime of faithfulness, skillful ministry, hard work, and loving his city, Bruce Wesley has become the unofficial gospel-centered Bishop of Houston. Our church is excited to be part of the collaboration of the church planting network and church planting residency his God-soaked vision has birthed. I pray other unofficial gospel-centered Bishops will emerge in cities around the world, working together to grow the Kingdom through the multiplication of churches!*

**Steve Bezner**
Senior Pastor, Houston NW Church

*"Collaboration for Multiplication" isn't just an incredible story of what God is doing in Houston, Texas, but it paints a wonderful picture of what true collaboration looks like in our cities. This book fueled my passion for reaching our city and inspired me to see the church collaborate around the mission of God in our city and geography. This is a must read for any city, movement and church planting leader focused on catalyzing a movement to reach your city through Kingdom collaboration, church planting and saturating your geography with the Gospel by multiplying and mobilizing the Church!*

**Chris Lagerlof**
Director of Mission Orange County (www.missionoc.org)

*Having spoken at a HCPN gathering and having seen the collaboration of Houston church planters in action, I left with a prayer in my heart for every city to have such a network. I believe God is using their efforts to reach an extremely diverse region and to encourage church planters and their wives, and I hope this idea, now written here in book form, will spark the creation of similar networks across the world.*

**Christine Hoover**
Author of The Church Planting Wife

# ACKNOWLEDGEMENTS

I dedicate this book to the church planters in the Greater Houston area.

## WITH THANKS TO...

### Exponential

Thank you, Todd and the Exponential team for providing a model for collaboration. I am honored that you asked me to contribute to Exponential's vision to accelerate the multiplication of healthy, reproducing churches.

### The Houston Church Planting Network

Thank you to the pastors and network leaders of HCPN. I appreciate your partnership (1) to encourage existing church planters; (2) to train church planters together; and (3) to ask God to create a church-planting movement that will bless Houston, Texas, and the world. Chad Clarkson, thank you for leading humbly and faithfully.

### ACTS 29

I am indebted to the pastors and executive board of the Acts 29 Network for modeling commitment and collaboration. I am grateful for your continued faithfulness to be a diverse global network of church-planting churches.

## AND FINALLY...

Thanks to the pastors and staff of Clear Creek Community Church who prevail by looking to Jesus. You inspire me by your generosity of spirit to serve church leaders.

Thank you to the people of Clear Creek Community Church for loving my family! I am able to give attention to church planting in Houston because of your devotion to the Kingdom of God. It's a joy to lock arms with you as we lead unchurched people to become fully devoted followers of Jesus. Let's keep telling the Great Story of the gospel and the stories of the people whose lives are changed by it. I love you.

Thanks to Byron Vaughn for your support throughout the writing process. Thanks to Pat Springle and Mandy Turner for editing the manuscript. And to my wife, Susan, thank you for your devotion to Jesus, your example of serving others and your ongoing encouragement.

# CONTENTS

# INTRODUCTION

I am an unlikely candidate to write on the topic of collaboration. If you compared the majority of my ministry efforts to a sport, I played on a golf team rather than a basketball team. I cheered for others but focused on my individual performance rather than teamwork.

Being overwhelmed changed me. I was overwhelmed by the number of lost people in Houston, Texas. I was overwhelmed by the vast Kingdom resources that never got utilized in the multiplication of disciples, churches and movements. I was overwhelmed by how long it takes and how much it costs to recruit, train, coach and resource a church planter to plant a church. How could we reach so many with the gospel with so few resources when it takes so long to prepare one church planter? This question changed me from thinking about ministry like a golf team to thinking about ministry like a basketball team. It changed my ministry from an individual activity to a team sport. I began to believe in collaboration.

The good people at Exponential asked me to write this book because I'm part of a group that has started two collaborative ministries in the last five years, both of which focus on multiplying churches. Together, we started doing ministry as a team sport.

The two ministries include the Houston Church Planting Network and The HCPN Collaborative Church Planting Residency. Because these two organizations are closely aligned and share the same name, let me differentiate them for you.

The Houston Church Planting Network is a gathering of people from multiple church-planting networks that meets nine times each year at lunch. We started HCPN as a place to strengthen church planters, to pray for the city, and to foster collaboration in church planting. HCPN does not plant churches. We do not fund church planters. We are just a gathering of people who do those things.

The HCPN Church Planting Residency is a yearlong finishing school for church planters who will plant in Houston, Texas. Uniquely, this residency is a collaborative work of a dozen diverse churches that come together to fund, train and support church planters that we hope will become movement leaders in Houston, Texas.

Evidently, collaboration of this sort is so rare that people want to hear about it when it happens. So this book is my attempt to tell how some church leaders in Houston began to practice collaboration for multiplication.

Chapter 1 tells **Our Story of Collaboration**. I write from my perspective, but the collective memory of other participants helped me string together experiences that God has woven into this story.

Chapter 2 examines **The Nine Tensions of Collaboration**. While learning to collaborate, we were reminded often of why it's difficult. In this chapter, I attempt to identify the tensions we faced and give some insights into how we navigated each one.

Chapter 3 is called **The Five Dynamics of Collaboration**. I offer no effort to make academic assertions about collaboration as a discipline. Rather, I seek to identify five things we learned that were so significant in our journey we want to keep doing them over and over again.

While writing, I was moved to worship repeatedly as God's kindness and providence shone throughout our story. I hope you will worship as you read, and I hope you will be compelled to give up the golf team and start doing ministry as a team sport. You can collaborate too.

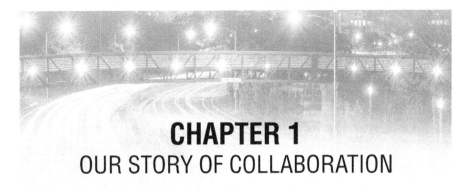

# CHAPTER 1
## OUR STORY OF COLLABORATION

The smell of Tex-Mex fills the former grocery store, now a fast-growing suburban church. The low roar is the sound of a couple hundred church planters, resource church pastors, and network leaders who have gathered for the monthly meeting of the Houston Church Planting Network (HCPN).

It's a diverse group gathered in the most ethnically diverse city in America, Houston, Texas. But the diversity does not stop there. At my table, there is a group of Assemblies of God pastors, a Presbyterian, a Baptist and an independent. They are only part of more than 30 different networks, some denominational and some not. The meeting format is pretty standard: lunch around the tables, informed praying for the sake of the city, and inspiring speakers to train and encourage church planters. Today, the speakers are local pastors. In previous gatherings, well-known pastors, authors and movement leaders have filled the platform.

The host pastor welcomes the group and reminds us, "The Houston Church Planting Network is a network of networks that exists to strengthen church planters who multiply churches to reach every man, woman and child in the greater Houston area." Even though I founded HCPN, I sometimes wonder how we got here.

### WHERE IT BEGAN

I vividly remember the first time I heard of a church-planting network. It was almost three decades ago. Steve and Paul Johnson were leading a session at a conference breakout. Each of the brothers had planted churches, one in Minnesota and one in Wisconsin. From the beginning, their new churches committed to raise up leaders and set aside a percentage of their offerings to plant other churches. The Johnsons demonstrated the power of multiplication—not only the power of multiplying disciples, but also the exponential power of multiplying churches. They painted a compelling picture of a raging wildfire of churches spreading across America and the world.

I had never met a church planter until that session in 1988. As a young pastor, my heart almost jumped out of my chest as I listened to these two men envision a viral movement of multiplying churches. With tears in my eyes, I breathed a prayer, *Dear God, let me be part of something like that in my lifetime.*

## STANDING ON THE SHOULDERS OF OTHERS

My first glimpse of a viral multiplication of churches was thrilling, and so was my first exposure to city-reaching movements. Jim Herrington and some other spiritual leaders in Houston started educating pastors about common ingredients of spiritual revivals that were sweeping through some cities of the world. Unified prayer and multiplying church-planting movements were two key ingredients. In Houston, church leaders spearheaded prayer meetings and retreats to ask God to transform our city. God used these prayer gatherings to tear down racial and denomination divisions in the city. While it wasn't really obvious at the time, it now seems that God had begun to answer our prayers.

## CLEAR CREEK COMMUNITY CHURCH

With my heart longing to be part of a church-planting movement in a city whose leaders cried out to God for spiritual renewal, we planted Clear Creek Community Church in the southeast quadrant of Houston in October 1993. We began with a few essential convictions:

- The church is God's people on God's mission.

- The mission of God, at least in part, is to seek and to save the lost.

- God's mission in the world would only be accomplished when God's people embrace His plan of multiplication.

The first vision documents of Clear Creek Community Church declared that we would plant 1,000 churches, beginning in the United States and reaching around the world. When people asked how we would do that, the answer was simple: through multiplication. Every church we planted would in turn plant other churches, which in turn would plant other churches, and so on.

## A SLOW START

One of the undeniable realities of multiplying movements is that they start slowly. Each generation requires years to develop. And not all church plants succeed, so the first harvest often comes slowly. The reality doesn't happen as consistently as the vision. The power of multiplying movements is not obvious in the short term. Only in the subsequent generations of a movement does the awe-inspiring power of multiplication emerge. Before we understood this principle, we had unrealistic expectations, and we grew discouraged in the earliest days of seeking to plant churches. We worked with a number of church planters and planted a church in Mexico, but we weren't seeing much progress toward our goal of 1,000 churches.

While church planting and multiplication was part of our rhetoric, the truth is that Clear Creek Community Church was growing rapidly. We were so busy managing our church's rapid growth that we didn't give much attention to the multiplication of churches. We focused on multiplying disciples, multiplying groups, and multiplying leaders, but not multiplying churches. We needed someone who would give leadership to our church-planting efforts.

In the first three years after moving into our first building, we had grown from 1,600 to 3,200 in weekend attendance. Each time we considered adding someone to our staff, there were significant staffing needs for those who would serve inside the church. *How could we spend the money and other resources on someone who didn't contribute directly to the obvious needs of our church's ministry?*

It began to dawn on me that this tension would never go away. At some point, we would have to decide if we would really be a Kingdom-minded church, or if we would settle for church growth. Would we learn to devote ourselves to the multiplication of other churches, or would we settle for only seeing people added to our local church?

## FINDING THE RIGHT LEADER

In 2005 we added Chad Clarkson to our staff as pastor of church planting and missions. Chad was a young, energetic leader with a penchant for networking. He had participated in multiple church plants in South Carolina, and the men he had partnered with were Kingdom-minded guys. Through them, God rooted in Chad's soul the values of Kingdom-building, city-reaching and multiplication. In hiring Chad, we had hit the mother lode.

However, the first few years at Clear Creek Community Church were frustrating for Chad. While we talked about church planting and multiplication, we didn't know how intoxicated we had become on the thrill of church growth. People love the feeling of being part of a really big thing. While church growth is good, church growth on its own becomes inward, competitive, stingy and self-absorbed.

Having Chad on staff exposed how often our choices in staffing, training, funding and celebrating were focused on ourselves. Little by little, his Kingdom-mindedness was the coffee that helped us sober up.

## BECOMING KINGDOM-MINDED

As we became more kingdom minded, our interest in multiplication piqued. Our staff read *Exponential* by Dave Ferguson and Jon Ferguson. (By the way, I'm not telling you this because the people at Exponential asked us to write this book. In the story of how Clear Creek Community Church became a Kingdom-minded, multiplying church, reading *Exponential* was catalytic.) Our staff read the book, and each staff person presented parts of the content for us to discuss. We focused on what multiplication looks like at every level of the church, and we gave ourselves to the development of leadership pipelines to raise up leaders who could help us multiply churches, campuses, groups and disciples. For us, reading and talking through *Exponential* was a game changer.

Just two years earlier, Clear Creek Community Church joined the Acts 29 Church Planting Network. While we were committed to planting churches, we had glaring limitations. Our church wasn't on the radar for most aspiring leaders, so we struggled to connect with potential church planters. Also, because we don't have a denominational focus, our circle of resources and shared learning was restricted. In short, we were too isolated to stay inspired. We needed partners around us who were solving the same problems, seeking the same outcomes and sharing what they learned along the way. In Acts 29, we found a tribe that shared our theological convictions and our missional priority: multiplication through church planting.

Becoming part of Acts 29 required a commitment to the membership covenant. Part of the covenant asks for a one-percent commitment to fund the operations of Acts 29 and a commitment to spend at least 10 percent of the church's general receipts on church planting. Acts 29 didn't seek to manage how churches spent their church-planting dollars; they only asked that every partner church make this commitment. Already, the Acts 29 Network was calling us to make the challenging commitment to be a church-planting church by putting our money where our mouth was. We did.

Networks are powerful; this was one of our greatest discoveries in our efforts to fulfill the Great Commission. In networks, you have relational reinforcements to keep you focused on the shared values that energize the network; in our case, the shared value is church planting. When we became part of Acts 29, we met more potential church planters; we invested more time and money in training church planters; and our vision for multiplying churches around the world was energized too. Credible networks overcome inertia. You get caught in the powerful current of the network's movement to plant churches.

While joining a church-planting network was helpful, I must admit that there was a learning curve for functioning effectively in it. While most organizational structures are top down, networks tend to be omnidirectional. The flow of information and new discoveries comes from anyone and everyone in the network, partly because the people in the network are not working to build the network as much as they are working on planting churches in and through their local context.

To give and receive, you have to show up in online conversations and at periodic gatherings to meet new people and share new discoveries. I couldn't just sit back and let things happen. I had to learn to initiate involvement in the network. Also, networks tend to be "low control and high accountability." Like NASCAR, you can have multiple stickers on your car. You can be involved in Acts 29 and in a denomination and still develop a city-reaching network in your local context—that's low control. But networks are relationally driven, so the high accountability comes from being face to face with other pastors who are in the trenches of everyday ministry while they're also committed to planting churches.

## GOD'S PROVIDENCE AND A PERFECT STORM

In retrospect, I see how God created the conditions for the perfect storm that led to the Houston Church Planting Network. The ingredients were all there:

- I had a latent desire to be part of a church-planting movement.
- The city of Houston had experienced the prayerful underpinnings of a city-reaching movement in the 1990s.
- God brought us a Kingdom-minded, operational leader in Chad Clarkson.
- We rediscovered multiplication through reading Exponential.
- We were caught up in the accelerating movement of the Acts 29 Network.

One more factor contributed to a powerful movement of God in our hearts. This time, it was theological.

One day when I was studying for a message, our teaching pastor, Yancey Arrington, burst through the door to my office. His intrusions weren't unusual, but this time it proved to be significant. Yancey pointed me to a message online by Tim Keller presented at The Gospel Coalition in 2009.

Keller recounted a story he had heard years before from Martyn Lloyd-Jones that demonstrated the difference between the gospel of Jesus and giving people good advice.

For reasons I can't explain, this message proved to be a watershed moment for Yancey and for me. Keep in mind, we are evangelical pastors who knew and preached the gospel of Jesus' substitutionary, atoning death on the cross and Jesus' powerful resurrection from the dead. We are essentially reformed in our theology, preaching salvation by grace alone through faith alone in Christ alone. But through Tim Keller's message and other books we read, we began to develop a fresh understanding that the gospel is central to our sanctification as well as our justification. The same grace that saved us also motivates us and empowers us to live fully submitted lives for God. This realization took us by storm.

Why was this renewal of gospel centrality relevant to the founding of the Houston Church Planting Network? We knew that any effort to create a network of churches that would cooperate for city transformation would require a unifying call beyond geography. Gospel centrality became that unifying call. Churches from different denominations, using different forms of governance, with different worship styles and diverse ethnic backgrounds could rally together to plant gospel-centered churches. The gospel of Jesus Christ was the centerpiece of our work together in the city.

God's preparation in my life for a church-planting network in the city had taken 20 years. I didn't know it at the time, but His sovereign grace had prepared me to initiate an interest meeting of pastors from across Houston to consider a partnership to plant churches. I had plenty of excuses to put it off: *I was too busy to do this. I had no detailed strategy. I didn't know what the outcome would be. Still, I felt compelled to start the conversation.*

We knew that other churches were committed to planting churches in Houston, but there was no cooperative effort that attempted to unify and multiply these efforts. How could we develop partnerships across the city?

## AN INVITATION TO COLLABORATION

With Chad Clarkson's help, I invited pastors from different ethnicities, denominations and traditions who had demonstrated any history of church planting to an interest meeting to consider partnering together to plant churches. Clear Creek Community Church hosted the meeting, which meant some people drove more than an hour to attend. We served a simple lunch; I gave a simple plea. The following was taken from my notes for the meeting in November 2009:

> *Our vision is a Church Planting Network for the City of Houston in which we cooperate to saturate the city with gospel-centered church plants, so that every man, woman, and child in Greater Houston has an opportunity to hear and respond to the Good News in the context of a faith community.*
>
> *Yesterday, I was in a room full of men who are part of a church-planting network, but their doctrinal distinctives and convictions about some practices might be too limiting for a group like the people in this room. I wonder if we can get on the same page with the following distinctives:*
>
> - *We are committed to reaching the city through saturation church planting.*
> - *We will focus on church planters who will plant gospel-centered churches.*
> - *We will communicate and cooperate about sharing our resources.*
>
> *We are standing on the shoulders of so many people and the work done by so many different groups. But no one has said, "We will take responsibility for church planting in the city." Who is going to take responsibility for the city? If not us, who?*

I announced that we would host a monthly gathering of church planters and resource church pastors to serve and strengthen church-planting efforts in the city. I invited people to join our efforts.

Frankly, the results of the meeting were thoroughly underwhelming. Many expressed their appreciation for lunch and voiced the need for new churches in the city, but differences loomed large. In the face of their reluctance, it seemed highly unlikely that pastors of larger churches would lead their congregations to reorient their efforts and resources to a new cooperative effort. But there were a few pastors of new and smaller churches who seemed genuinely interested.

A monthly gathering for lunch and encouragement began immediately. We asked churches to host who were closer to the center of the city. We intentionally sought to put other people up front so that the experience didn't feel like it was all about Clear Creek Community Church. While the church planters who attended seemed grateful, this wasn't much of a movement. We had little traction. Chad Clarkson was carrying the organizational burden, and Clear Creek Community Church was footing the bill.

This inertia and lethargy lasted more than a year. At times, we wondered if we should just give up. *After all, we're a suburban church. We aren't really in the city of Houston. Maybe a city-reaching effort or church-planting movement would have to come from a church in the city.* But we continued to provide monthly meetings to encourage church planters and invite participation from networks across the city.

## UNEXPECTED LESSONS

Our efforts to get some traction led in two directions. First, Chad continued to meet with network leaders across the city. He built trust. He asked how the Houston Church Planting Network could serve the leaders and their networks. When we gathered, he put the microphone in other leaders' hands. Second, I worked with a few interested young leaders to create a strategic design for the Houston Church Planting Network. Chuck Land, Chad Karger, Mitch Maher, Bryant Lee, Chad Clarkson and I crafted the following mission statement: *The Houston Church Planting Network exists as a network of networks to strengthen church planters to multiply churches that reach every man, woman and child in the greater Houston area.*

We set three objectives for our gatherings: We will (1) understand and pray for our city; (2) encourage church planters; and (3) facilitate collaboration. Slowly, we began to get traction.

Simultaneously, Clear Creek Community Church invested more deeply in training church planters. We started a coaching center for church planters that focused on two topics: leadership and missional ecclesiology. We believe church planters must be equipped as leaders because they are starting something from the ground up. And we believe church planters must be missionaries who see the church as "God's sent people" so the church will be focused on the Great Commission.

The leadership content came from the Leadership Development Program we developed at our church. The missiology content came from Dwight Smith's workbook, Renovation. Church planters gathered two mornings a month with Chad and other leaders from our church to be coached. We used the coaching center format for four consecutive years to train 17 church planters, which resulted in 15 churches being planted in the Greater Houston area.

The coaching center resulted in three unforeseen benefits. First, we expected to see churches planted, but we didn't foresee the growing credibility we would gain with church leaders across the city. Second, we didn't foresee the growing sense of partnership that would come from the stories told by the church planters we trained. With these men in the room each time the Houston Church Planting Network gathered, the sense of partnership was palpable. And third, the coaching center also prepared us to begin a church planters residency program at Clear Creek Community Church in 2012.

The residency was more comprehensive and intensive than the coaching center. We provided space for men to have an office together at our campus. They spent half of their time learning and the other half working in the community where they would plant their churches. Over a period of 10 months, we focused on 11 core competencies of a church planter. After two years of providing the residency program, we had trained nine men who planted seven more churches. From this progress, we gained more trust from other church leaders across the city too.

Credibility is built over time. In the beginning, we didn't know that we would have to demonstrate unfiltered and unilateral commitment over time by doing this work alone before others would feel compelled to do this work together. So for six years, we trained church planters. For four years, Clear Creek Community Church funded and led the Houston Church Planting Network. Little by little, we included the periodic help of churches who hosted the monthly gathering and provided lunch. Finally, we began to see a growing level of collaboration. "You" turned to "we" when talking about HCPN. In year five, it was time to take a next step.

## CASTING A VISION FOR THE CITY

In fall 2013, I again cast a vision for reaching Houston through planting churches. I gave people a brief sketch of the beauty and brokenness of our city. I told the leaders that Houston is growing by a megachurch per week. It's the most ethnically diverse city in America with more than 220 languages and over 350 people groups. We have more than 1 million foreign-born citizens. We have a booming economy and a long line of accolades. But Houston also has a dark side. It is a hub for sex traffickers and modern-day slavery. We are home to one of the largest abortion clinics in the world. We are the most income-segregated of the 10 largest U.S. cities. Childhood health in Houston ranks at the bottom of national averages. While we have more megachurches than any other U.S. city, big lighthouses aren't sufficient to light our large, dark and diverse city. It won't be big churches that transform Houston, but rather hundreds of small churches carrying light into every dark corner of the city.

At the HCPN meeting, I cast a vision for us to make planting churches a shared commitment in our efforts to reach the city:

"Church planting is a core commitment for evangelization of our city, for the transformation of our churches, and for the transformation of our city.

"Our vision is to develop a community of leaders committed to a multiplying movement of missional churches to plant churches in the Greater Houston Area. We want to fulfill the Great Commission: so that every man, woman and child in the Greater Houston area will have the opportunity to hear and respond to the Good News in the context of a faith community, and we want to transform the city by serving the city as sent people."

The conclusion will give you a feel for the vision talk. Below is an excerpt from my manuscript.

> *Great movement in the city is not about giant or large churches or TV pastors, but the wildfire of the gospel-centered and missional churches multiplying throughout the city. It will not be like an elephant, but like a field of mice. It will be an infestation.*
>
> *I see 15-year-old boys and girls catching a vision for planting churches in the city. I see them being trained from their teenage years; I see an army being raised up for the sake of God's church in the city.*
>
> *I see churches accepting geographical responsibility for every man, woman and child in their circle of concern. The spark and the fire of WoodsEdge and Houston Northwest and Sojourn and First Pres and Kingsland Baptist become commonplace. And the flame is lit in the hearts of men and women who carry the fire to another church plant in another geography.*
>
> *I see dead and dying churches resurrected to the mission of Jesus. Twenty years ago I pastored a church just outside Loop 610. The community was declining then, but it's on the verge of rebound now. And God raised up men who were playing in the backyard and crying to Mama over skinned knees at that time, to be His men to raise up a people for Himself in that community.*
>
> *I see pastors of large resource churches, rich churches who can't ignore the blaze of God in the city, awakened in the night by the Holy Spirit who is prodding them, compelling them to take the steps, to invest the resources, to risk it all for the sake of the gospel in the city. In order for this to happen, an emerging collective identity must take root in us. What does this collective identity look like?*
>
> *We are **missionaries**. We are people redeemed and sent by a missional God to advance His Kingdom through the planting of healthy, gospel-centered churches. We are a community of church planters who know*

*and love Jesus, who know and love our communities, and who are captivated with the beauty, power, and centrality of the local church. We are committed to reaching people who don't have a relationship to Jesus. We are the friends of sinners just like our Savior.*

*We preach a gospel that declares God has done for us what we could not do for ourselves, a gospel that reminds us that we are more sinful than we imagined and more loved than we ever thought possible. We preach the story of a sinless Savior, who died a horrible death in our place on a Roman cross. Who died and was buried for three days and who rose victoriously over sin and death and hell. We preach a gospel that is not shocked by sin, or threatened by darkness, or subject to hopelessness. We preach a gospel of grace that we will not allow to be tainted by legalism, or twisted by moralism or marginalized by religion. We preach a gospel that is the power of God unto salvation, a gospel that changes hearts, homes, marriages, businesses, affections, value systems and cultures. As "sent people," we preach God's gospel. So we have no power of our own, we have no message of our own—we live dependent on the Spirit and we listen for the One Voice that will change our direction in an instant. We are committed to multiplying disciples, groups, leaders, churches and movements.*

*God did not intend for us to do this on our own, so we are compelled to walk together. And we should walk together. After all, it's part of our identity.*

*We are **brothers**. We are common sons of our Heavenly Father, the Most High God. Our Father's love for us is the means and measure of our love for one another. No one walks alone. We depend on one another, we defend one another, we help one another, and we speak the truth in love to one another. Each one of us has brothers we can call for a lifeline. We are a brotherhood of godly men because we are like our Father, healthy men because our Father's way gives life, and trustworthy men because faithfulness runs in the family.*

*We are not competitors, critics, cynics, or scoffers. We do not talk about one another; we talk to one another. We are not sissified and overly* sensitive and we are not given to bravado or competition. Rather, we are sober and supportive. My success is your success, and your success is my success. After all, we are about the family business. So unlike competition in the business world, we embrace collaboration. We celebrate each other's successes. We support one another. We defer to one another. We are brothers. So we are missionaries and we are brothers.

Finally, we are **stewards**. As stewards, the Father has entrusted to us the oversight and management of His most precious resources. These things are not ours; they are His, but He has entrusted them to us. He entrusted the gospel to us; we are stewards of the gospel. He entrusted relationships to us; we are stewards of relationships. He entrusted opportunities to us; we are stewards of what we learn. He entrusted young men to us. We are stewards of the men God has called to plant churches. As stewards, we are committed to managing what God has given us so we can plant healthy, gospel-centered churches through coaching relationships and collaborative residencies.

We need men who will commit to lead a multiplying movement of missional churches to plant churches in the Greater Houston area. We need men who will carry the burden, cast the vision, pray earnest prayers, equip qualified men to pastor, and who will believe that on our watch and in our lifetime, God will do something in this city that we will speak about in humbled tones in heaven.

We need people who believe that in our lifetime God will transform a life. And God will release an infestation of new churches across the city that will love their way into every corner of human brokenness with Good News and good deeds. God will restore His church to bring Shalom to a city in such a way that Christians believe it can happen again, and they will cry out all over the world, "Do it again, Lord!" And He will do it in such a way that it will not be about any of us, but it will cause nations to sing His praise.

The vision I cast that day was not new. I was singing the same song we had been singing for four years, but others finally began to sing along. After my talk, pastors and leaders from many churches expressed interest in collaborating together to plant churches. People asked for my notes;

others wanted me to talk to their group of pastors. What I hoped would happen four years earlier when we gathered for the first HCPN meeting was finally happening. A wave was coming our way.

## CATCHING THE WAVE

When a wave comes, you have to catch it. In fall 2013, we could feel the swell of enthusiasm about partnering to plant churches for the sake of the city. We decided to hold an interest meeting immediately after the January gathering of HCPN. At the meeting, we planned to boldly ask pastors to lead their churches to join with us in a collaborative church-planting residency.

Coordinating a meeting of senior pastors and missions pastors from various denominations and ethnicities is no small feat. In retrospect, it wouldn't have happened without the commitment of two men who were new friends. Chad Clarkson developed a friendship with Jeremiah Morris, an associate pastor from First Presbyterian Church in Houston. Together, Chad and Jeremiah personally invited potential partners from across the city to gather in a meeting where I would cast a vision for collaboration.

Alan Hirsch was the guest speaker for the Houston Church Planting Network meeting in January 2014. Around 200 participants heard Hirsch's compelling call for churches to function in the way Paul described in Ephesians 4. Truthfully, before Alan finished his talk, my mind was swirling around what was about to happen. The butterflies in my stomach reminded me that deep inside I knew the meeting that I was about to lead was ripe with Kingdom potential.

After Alan's closing prayer, I moved quickly to the conference room in First Presbyterian Church. Men representing eight churches encircled the long table. From the end of the table, I ran my simple slide show to remind people of the need in our city. I reviewed the history of planting churches through the coaching center and residency at Clear Creek Community Church. Then I made the big ask.

## THE BIG ASK

I asked the pastors to join us in a collaborative church-planting residency program for the sake of the city. I said that our goal was not to simply develop a residency, but to collaborate in a way that we can multiply residencies that multiply churches across the city. To multiply, we needed to agree that we wouldn't treat anything as proprietary, but rather we would share as openly as possible with the hope that God might use His work among us to bless other cities too. Affirming nods filled the room with agreement, so I rolled out the straw-man strategy as follows:

- The collaborative residency will be a cohort of eight to 12 church planters enlisted from around the country.

- We will want to find outstanding leaders to participate in the residency. We will pay them a stipend of $50,000 for the year.

- The men will be trained and resourced by churches from across the city. Some older churches with financial resources will serve as anchor churches, and new church plants will serve as training grounds for the church planters.

- The collaborative residency will not be a pastoral residency, but a church-planting residency for men who will plant in the Greater Houston area within a year.

- Each church planter will be tethered to an anchor church and a new church plant; those connections will be guided by shared theological distinctives.

- We will have four objectives. The cohort of church planters will (1) be trained in keeping with 11 core competencies; (2) form deep community through weekly soul care together; (3) establish relationships with spiritual leaders in the city; and (4) develop the prospectus and core of the churches to be planted.

- Participating pastors commit to be personally involved in the training of church planters at some level and to host the church planters and their wives at least one time in the anchor pastor's home too.

- Finally, pastors would agree to pray for the church planters and support the vision of multiplying churches to reach the city.

I assured the pastors around the table, "This is not a Clear Creek Community Church thing." Even though we would give leadership to the development of the training based on years of experience, we knew the residency required an identity that was larger than any one church. We would house the residency as close as possible to the center of the city. A board of directors would be comprised of anchor church pastors or a representative assigned by the anchor churches. The structure and our language would demonstrate that this is a truly collaborative work instead of being a ministry of Clear Creek Community Church.

Then I explained the financial model, "Anchor churches will contribute $100,000 per year for the collaborative residency." I was proud of myself for saying that without flinching. I knew it was a big ask; and yet I also knew that Clear Creek Community Church would lead the way in generosity. Other churches can participate at varying levels too. The tiered funding model invited participation of churches of various sizes, ages and capacities for giving. The $700,000 budget covered the stipend for the residents, the recruiting and training expenses, and the salary of the residency director.

When I asked for questions, it was clear that we had not thought of everything. We were most unclear about the relationship between the participants and their anchor church. This would prove to be a tension point as the residency unfolded. We also had no plan for how we would receive funds, or whether anchor churches could select their own participants, or how the church planters would be funded after the residency. In spite of not knowing the answers to all of their questions, the eagerness in the room was palpable.

Actually, for some of the pastors in the room, this wasn't the first time they had heard we would be asking them for a significant investment to fund the residency. When Jeremiah and Chad talked with several of them to share the vision and stoke the fire, they explained that involvement included a measure of funding. When I asked the pastors to give generously to our collaborative work, they were ready, willing and able.

## ESSENTIALS FOR COLLABORATION

The dialogue that followed revealed five essentials for collaboration. Jim Birchfield, the senior pastor of Houston's First Presbyterian Church, spoke up. He said that First Presbyterian, the oldest church in Texas, had planted at least 15 churches in its storied history, but the church had not planted a church in the last 20-plus years. He said they would definitely commit to this work as a way of seeing God renew the missional impulse of First Presbyterian Church. *The first essential for collaboration is a shared conviction that church planting is essential to reach the city.*

A second essential emerged from the experience of Jeff Wells, the founding and senior pastor of WoodsEdge Community Church in The Woodlands. Jeff told of how his church had focused on prayer and international church planting for years. Independent from HCPN, they had sensed a fresh call of God to turn more of their attention to the city of Houston. They were ready to commit to the collaborative residency also. *The second essential for collaboration is a call from God.*

Blake Wilson, the founding and lead pastor at Crossover Bible Church was the only African-American pastor in the room. He explained the challenges of church planting in the African-American church culture. *We realized the third essential for collaboration is sensitivity to cultural differences in the churches of ethnic minorities.* Crossover Bible Church committed to participate at some level.

Almost five years of monthly gatherings helped build relational trust and affection between us. Jeff Wells and I would spend the first year deepening the relationships of pastors by sharing lunch together and meeting quarterly to review our progress as a residency. *Relationship is the fourth essential for collaboration.*

The most important of the five essentials for collaboration emerged around theological questions. Ken Werlein, the founding and senior pastor at Faithbridge Church along with Executive Pastor Brian McGown, participated in the first formative meetings. They recognized that the participating churches were predominantly reformed in their theology. They asked, "Are we going to be treated like the 'step child' since we are

Wesleyan?" Everyone in the room was aware of the weight of the question. Could we collaborate in spite of differing theological convictions?

We determined that the gospel is our meeting place. *The gospel, then, is the fifth and most profound essential for collaboration.*

We clarified the gospel as Good News of God's grace in the substitutionary death of Jesus to atone for the sins of man and His bodily resurrection from the dead. Moreover, God's Good News is that salvation is by grace through faith in Jesus; it is not merited by good works or religious deeds. We could agree that this gospel is the theological core of our cooperative efforts and the message that we want the churches planted to push into every dark corner of our city. The gospel is the theological sameness that we build on while theological differences would be addressed by assigning participants to anchor churches and church plants according to theological distinctives.

## FINANCIAL COMMITMENTS

We hoped each of the five churches would commit to give $100,000 each to start HCPN while a dozen or more other churches might give less. Within a few weeks of the vision- casting meeting at First Presbyterian Church, four churches had committed to give $100,000, another committed $50,000, and others gave lesser amounts, but with a commitment to increase their commitment as they were able. As word got out, additional established churches and dozens of church plants made commitments too.

Houston's First Baptist Church became an anchor church with a $100,000 commitment. When I received word of their participation, I recalled a lunch with their pastor, Greg Matte, some five years earlier. Then, the timing wasn't right for collaboration. Houston's First Baptist, with their rich history of generosity toward mission ventures in the city and around the world, had then been on the front end of a major initiative. But now the timing was right, which was another reminder of God's providence to bring our work together.

We saw something remarkable happening: In these churches, different visions, histories and callings were coming together. What God had been sowing in churches and pastors was beginning to grow. It's not that we didn't work hard, but it was obvious that God was moving in leaders' hearts' and in their churches to be part of something bigger than what they could accomplish by themselves. It was time for action.

## FORMATIVE EFFORTS

Fortunately, we soon discovered that the leaders of the participating churches are people of action—they don't spend too much time deliberating before they make bold moves. If they had been too cautious or too reluctant, I'm not sure anything would have happened. We needed a good blend of creativity, boldness and wisdom because we were making it up as we went along.

In a few initial gatherings, we were satisfied with high-level direction from the board and formative action by the director, Chad Clarkson, along with Jeremiah Morris. The board reviewed documents and shared comments by email, and Chad ran hard. We tried to learn from as many people as we could as well, so we determined to take a trip to Little Rock, Arkansas, to learn from Bill Wellons and John Bryson with Fellowship Associates.

For 18 years, Bill has led Fellowship Associates to train movement-leading church planters. We believe Fellowship Associates is the premier residency program in the country. Bill and John were generous with their experience and coaching; the one-day trip shaped the HCPN Church Planting Residency in multiple ways. Among other insights, Bill said the cohort experience is key to the residency training, with a cohort of six to eight being optimal. Also, the training itself must be shaped to the needs of the cohort. I intended for the training materials to be predetermined, but Bill urged us to be clear on our objectives while still retaining the flexibility to address the specific needs of each individual. And to our great benefit, Chad Clarkson entered a coaching relationship with Bill.

## RECRUITING THE FIRST CLASS OF RESIDENTS

The first great challenge was recruiting the initial class of church-planting residents. We limited candidates to men for two reasons: the emphasis on a learning cohort required a level of openness that happens best with people of the same gender, and the theological position of some of the churches limits eldership to men. After recruiting church-planting residents for almost two decades, Bill Wellons and John Bryson urged us to recruit men in their late 20s to early 30s who had ministry experience, a history of proven leadership, and an experience with some kind of brokenness. Our experience at recruiting residents for Clear Creek Community Church informed our commitment to assess men according to 11 core competencies and a clearly articulated call from God to plant a church in the Greater Houston area.

The next step included a full court press to get the word out about the HCPN Church Planting Residency. A leading ad agency, MMI, laid the groundwork pro bono with a press release, brochures and an updated website. We urged anchor churches to utilize every network, denomination and educational connection to recruit. Seminary leaders allowed me to cast our vision at an annual luncheon. The surprise in the recruiting process turned out to be the former residents at Clear Creek Community Church who remained connected to HCPN.

The recruitment process included the following steps:

1. **Online assessment**
   We used a helpful tool created by Gateway Church in Austin called *Church Planter Profiles*. Candidates complete this assessment and then send us a resume with a family photo.

2. **Resume and Family Photo**
   A family photo is a picture that paints a thousand words. Is the candidate playful, serious, perfectionistic, artistic, or casual? Everything is data when seeking to discern the best men for the residency.

3. **Interview Call**
   The focus of the call is to evaluate the person's competencies and general readiness to plant a church. Did he return calls quickly? Was he professional in the conversation? Did he seem transparent or guarded? Was he humble and responsive, or did he talk too much? The call was where we began to say, "no" and "not yet" to people, because what follows the call is a time-consuming application. We

didn't want to waste a candidate's time completing the application (or our time reading it) if he didn't look like a viable candidate.

**4. Extensive Application**

The application includes detailed information about the candidate's family, their individual story, and their ministry and leadership experience. We also ask theological questions and ask for their responses to hypothetical but very common challenges in ministry.

**5. Additional Testing and Assessments**

We use multiple tests to discern important patterns in a candidate's life. We use StrengthFinders, Golden Personality, Portrait Predictor, a spiritual gifts assessment, churchplanterprofiles.com and 360 interviews.

**6. Candidate and Spouse Personal Assessment**

Three or four HCPN partners conduct the formal assessment. We include at least one assessor from the potential anchor church to assist the church's decision of whether or not they will embrace this candidate as their resident and work with him throughout the year.

**7. Candidate's Packets Sent to Residency Team**

Lead pastors and church representatives review the packets with detailed notes about each candidate. They listen to recorded sermons. After a lot of prayer and deliberation, they decide on the class of residents. Influencing factors include a love for Houston, a sense of calling, ministry experience, ability to connect with the cohort, leadership history, marital health, potential to multiply other leaders and a general sense of authentic spirituality.

In selecting the first class of residents, Chad Clarkson considered more than 60 men to recruit seven residents. The criteria made it easy to say "no" to some and "not yet" to others. We were looking for men who were 12 to 18 months from planting a church. Some potential candidates needed a longer runway than HCPN would provide. We consider HCPN a "finishing" residency, while other programs are "foundational" residencies; their objective is to lay a foundation for ministry. Still others are "functional" residencies with the objective of allowing someone to serve with them so they can learn how a particular ministry functions. Foundational residencies teach the many possible styles of ministry.

Functional residencies demonstrate a single style of ministry. Finishing residencies must help church planters design their style of ministry.

## BUILDING THE BRIDGE AS WE WALK ACROSS IT

You might think we started the HCPN Church Planting Residency with a refined and tested curriculum. Nope, we didn't. We decided we would build the bridge as we walked across it. We had years of experience training church planters, and we had some clear objectives, which we always keep clear. As a reminder, *The cohort of church planters will (1) be trained in keeping with 11 core competencies, (2) form deep community through weekly soul care together, (3) establish relationships with spiritual leaders in the city, and (4) develop the prospectus and launch team of the churches to be planted.*

The core competencies include:

Spiritual Vitality

Theological Clarity

Conviction

Marriage and Family

Relationships

Leadership

Maturity

Missional Lifestyle

Disciple Making

Ability to Teach

Entrepreneurial Aptitude

The residency started with a retreat where residents discovered that church planting is not just about skills; it's about heart. We asked penetrating questions: What unresolved issues abide in you? What are your sin patterns? What idols surface in your life? How do you deal with conflict? How do you press the gospel into others and yourself? How emotionally available and connected are you? Are you appropriately transparent? Are you authentic? We all realized that focusing on the heart is the best way to deepen relationships in a cohort and begin a yearlong residency.

Chad Clarkson, Jeremiah Morris and Chad Karger oversee the weekly flow of the residency. The rhythm includes class time together on Tuesday and Thursday. Tuesdays focus on soul care; Thursdays focus on skill development. On Mondays and Wednesdays, residents learn from the participating churches and develop their own launch team. They identify, research and engage with their circle of accountability in the geography where they will plant their churches.

Each lead pastor of the anchor churches hosts the residents and their wives in his home to build rapport and discuss important issues related to marriage and family in pastoral ministry. Pastors also focus on training in their particular areas of strength or expertise, including prayer, strategic leadership, preaching and missional engagement.

We bring in experts for some training topics. Will Mancini, author of Church Unique, trains the residents through his Vision Co::lab. In these exercises, residents develop their vision frame: mission, vision, values, measures and strategies. Will provides follow-up calls with each resident. Other experts train residents in fundraising, preaching skills and launch team development.

As I write, it's too early to tell if the bridge we're building is actually going to get residents to a place where they're equipped to plant a church and thrive in the process. We might not be sure how we'll get there, but we can already see the destination from here.

Did you see yourself in our story thus far? I hope so. And I hope you were inspired to leverage your gifts and your relationships to collaborate with others to train church planters and to plant multiplying churches in your context. If you plan to take a next step, be sure to read the next chapter to learn about some of the tensions you might encounter as you collaborate to multiply.

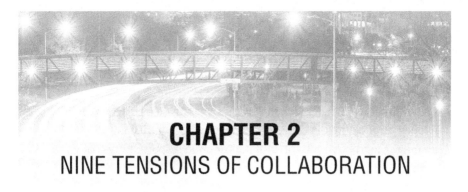

# CHAPTER 2
## NINE TENSIONS OF COLLABORATION

The old adage goes, "If it was easy, everyone would do it." We usually hear this when we feel the pain associated with doing something worthwhile, but difficult. Collaboration fits here. It's worthwhile, but difficult. But why is it difficult to get churches who share the same Lord, and the same Great Commission and, in our case, the same city, to collaborate? One might think that collaboration would come naturally to us. In this chapter, I want to address the nine tensions of collaboration.

## THE LOCAL CHURCH VS. THE CHURCH IN THE CITY

As I sat at the table with senior pastors of growing churches to share our vision, I couldn't help but wonder how they would receive my call to join together in a work to bless the city through planting new churches.

Because I had experienced tension regarding the nature of the church, I imagined they had the same questions. Is the church a local body of baptized Christ followers who share a common mission, who submit to recognized leaders, observe ordinances together, gather regularly to encourage one another and worship? If so, that is church with a little c. Or is the church the body of Christ in the city, people from different churches all across the city with a common faith in Jesus, and a shared responsibility to herald the gospel in word and deed to bless the city? Are we one church that meets in different congregations across the city with a joint responsibility? That's the Church with a big C.

The New Testament includes references to both the big C and the little c. Some pastors and teachers emphasize the collective identity of the church in the city, the big C. The letters to the Galatians, the Philippians and the Corinthians were addressed to Christians in a city who made up the church in that city. In the Book of Revelation, John refers to the churches in Asia Minor as a people with a common identity. In each city, the church received a common rebuke and discipline. The church in Ephesus had left her first love. The church in Thyatira tolerated a false teacher. God set an open door before the church at Philadelphia. In each community, their common geography brought with it a common responsibility that gave them a common identity.

Some say, "See, it's one church in each city." But is it that way because there was only one congregation in the city, or because the writers of the New Testament believed that all the Christians of many congregations in the city made up one church?

Those who emphasize the autonomy of each local church say that most of the references to the church in the New Testament are focused on distinct local congregations. Each had elders who were distinct from those in other congregations, and each group of elders was responsible to nurture and discipline the disciples in that particular local church. This emphasis of the local congregation, little c church, was the common perspective around the table of pastors to whom I was casting a vision for collaboration.

These men served as pastors of distinct local congregations. Even if these pastors embraced the belief that there is one church in the city, their experience in the local church reinforced a strong sense of autonomy. Approval and participation in our residency program would come in different ways depending on the church, so we had to collaborate in a way that maintained autonomy while still promoting shared responsibility.

Consequently, I didn't try to redefine the nature of the church as being one church in the city. That point of view might have derailed our conversation and positioned me wrongly and inaccurately as someone with a hobbyhorse that I wanted everyone else to ride. Instead, I focused on what we had in common: the lostness of our city and the Great Commission of our Lord. I celebrated our common desires, emphasizing how collaboration would glorify God and strengthen our ability to bless the city through planting churches. I suggested that each of our autonomous congregations could celebrate the success of our common labors as the fruit of their local church, which leads to another tension.

## MY CHURCH PLANT VS. OUR CHURCH PLANT

As we collaborate to plant churches in the city, one of the questions asked most often is, "Whose church plant is this?" Sometimes the question relates to who will take ultimate responsibility for the new church. More often, however, the question centers on who gets credit for the new church plant. On the surface, this sounds more selfish than it really is. Churches who are cooperating to plant churches for the first time feel responsible to report the outcomes of their mission gifts with integrity. If we give credit for each church plant to all participating churches, the accounting seems off.

Multiplication requires that we get beyond the issue of who gets credit for a church plant. HCPN churches determined to create a different way to report our progress, so we changed the way we keep score. We decided to report what we do together instead of reporting what we do apart. The reporting itself calls for a new perspective for many of the participating churches regarding mission. Now, we see our calling as collaborative work, and we celebrate results as collaborative fruit. In this way, we all take the credit together, and none of us take the credit alone.

## HAVING A VOTE VS. HAVING A VOICE

The HCPN Church Planting Residency is made up of a dozen contributing churches. So how are we to make decisions? Who gets to sit at the table, and what gets them there? After all, everyone is contributing time and money.

From the start of HCPN, we knew that the entire effort was vulnerable at the point of polity. We determined not to get gridlocked in a cumbersome political process to select candidates or assign church-planting residents to churches. We determined that while every contributing church has a voice, but not everyone has a vote.

Each church shapes the residency program by their interaction with the executive director and the residents themselves, so their voice is heard. But the HCPN Executive Board is the governing body, made up of the lead pastors of the anchor churches and selected pastors whose involvement will keep the residency sensitive to the needs of ethnic minorities.

## FAIR FUNDING VS. SACRIFICIAL FUNDING

Collaboration often assumes equitable requirements and a fair distribution of benefits. Why should one church pay more or do more than another church if both churches receive the same benefits from a residency program? Of course, this question misses the spirit of the kind of true collaboration we practice.

Sacrifice trumps fairness every time. Sacrificial funding is required for collaboration to begin. Someone has to commit their resources first, and they might have to commit for a number of years before enough trust is built for others to participate. In this spirit, Clear Creek Community Church funded HCPN for years, and then, others began to generously contribute too. Participants fund at various contribution levels. Each participant, regardless of the level of their giving, begins to feel part of the team and celebrates successes together. This spirit of collaboration changes the culture in the room when HCPN gathers. We are co-laborers for the city. So we don't require equitable giving. The standard in multiplying movements isn't fairness; it's sacrifice.

## KEEPING LEADERS VS. RELEASING LEADERS

At this writing, we are celebrating Chad's 10th anniversary on our staff at Clear Creek Community Church as the pastor of church planting and missions. His profound impact on our local church is seen in church-planter coaching centers, international church-planting partnerships, small groups engaging the community with the gospel, and a general sense of people identifying themselves as missionaries in their local context. So the thought of Chad giving 80 percent of his time to direct the HCPN Church Planting Residency felt a little like cutting off an arm.

Every pastor decides whether to be Kingdom-minded or to focus on growing the local church. Some of the decisions to be Kingdom-minded are more painful than others. It's not so hard to pray for God's work outside your local context or to set aside 10 percent or more of your budget for God's work outside your church. But when impact players shift most of their focus from your local congregation to the work of the larger church, the cost of Kingdom collaboration seems really expensive. The more that staff positions contribute to equipping and assisting those outside the church, the more stress we feel inside the church. In these moments, you realize what you really believe about multiplication.

When Chad started spending most of his time working with HCPN, we were without our established leader of local and global missions at Clear Creek Community Church. His assistant bore much of the burden, but many of our small groups felt his absence when he wasn't available to respond to questions or guide local mission efforts. Are we glad we made this move with Chad? It depends on what day you ask.

We didn't capriciously shift Chad's role to lead the HCPN Church Planting Residency; we planned and considered the possibility for years. Chad knew this shift would require that he equip leaders to oversee each area of ministry for which he was responsible.  Equipping others to take oversight is not as urgent if churches are simply focused on church growth. After all, the staff person is there for oversight.

But when you're committed to multiplication, people equip and deploy others into the multiplying work of the Kingdom with an appropriate sense of desperation. There are increasing numbers of campuses, churches and projects that need new leaders. It's part and parcel to how the Kingdom grows. So Kingdom-minded churches choose to equip and release leaders so that the Kingdom grows, even if at times the church feels the pinch. Sometimes the pinch created by collaboration isn't related to the people we release. Instead, it's a time pinch felt by the Kingdom-minded pastor.

## A PASTOR WHO LEADS A CHURCH VS. A PASTOR WHO LEADS IN THE CITY

The tension that I feel most intensely about multiplication through collaborating with other churches for the sake of the city relates to my time. Most pastors are already too busy with local church responsibilities. Who has time for something else?

Today, I left the office in the middle of a time blocked out to prepare messages to attend a gathering of HCPN pastors in the city. I treat study times as sacred to be prepared each time I preach. I rarely allow anything to interrupt a block of study, but I did today. The commute to the HCPN meeting was 50 minutes each way, and the meeting was three hours long. Participating in the gathering today required almost five hours of my day. If the HCPN Board had met today as it does sometimes before regular meetings, it would have taken even more time. Almost every time I do something with HCPN, it means that I'm taking time away from my responsibilities at Clear Creek Community Church. Whenever you say "yes" to something, you always say "no" to something else.

Why would our elders allow me to use 20 percent of my time to work with groups outside of Clear Creek Community Church? Ultimately, we feel responsible to God not only for what happens at Clear Creek Community Church, but for what happens in our city too. Of course, we aren't solely responsible for Houston, but we are jointly responsible. We can't ignore the need for multiplying leaders and churches, and we can't leave it to someone else. We believe that God has called us to rearrange our priorities to include collaboration with others for the sake of this city. We make time for what we believe is important and for things for which we are responsible.

## FORMATIVE PARTNERS VS. NEW PARTNERS

Multiplication demands that when a movement gets traction, it necessarily welcomes new partners. But new partners create tension. The new partners want to shape the direction of the collaborative work. Also, getting people on board takes time. You have to recast the vision, retell the collective narrative and restate the values and purpose of collaboration. New partners might change the relational dynamics, or they might bring onerous expectations or previous relational conflicts or trust gaps. In spite of these potential tensions, multiplying movements go beyond simply adding partners; multiplying movements actively recruit new partners.

Why do we invite the added stress of new partners? The HCPN Church Planting Residency recruits and adds new partners because we want to see far more churches planted across the city. We have already begun to equip new residencies in specific parts of the city, and we aspire to create different types of church-planting residencies for future church planters who need a longer season of preparation. New partners provide the energy and resources for growth, and they bring new relational pipelines for collaboration.

So how do we maximize the benefits of new partners and minimize the tensions? Collaborative efforts like HCPN must develop an onboarding process for new partners similar to the way many churches onboard new members. We share the need, cast a vision, declare expectations and ask for specific commitments that will keep our collaboration healthy. For various reasons, some churches need more time before they can commit to wholehearted collaboration. They have to wait for another budget cycle, they are waiting for other leaders to become supportive, or their particular season of church life makes new commitments unreasonable. We don't pressure people. We simply continue to invite their participation if and when the time seems right for them.

## A SHARED STORY VS. A SHARED STRATEGY

Developing collaborative partnership requires both a shared story and a shared strategy. The tension surfaces over which comes first.

Story is more compelling to collaborative partners than strategy. A shared story is the recognition of God's work around us, told in a connected narrative that demonstrates God's providential work in the city. In a well-articulated shared story, listeners can see their place in God's work in the city. There is a powerful and compelling sense that we are caught up in something together to accomplish the purposes of God.

Strategy is less collaborative by nature. Usually, someone is the mastermind behind a strategy. Partners are invited to share the load in building out a plan with shared responsibilities. Strategies are good and necessary, but strategies don't feel organic. In fact, they often feel contrived. That doesn't mean they're wrong or evil—strategy is necessary to give clarity of vision and to chart the path of shared leadership and common commitment. But multiplying leaders who build collaborative partnerships get the order right: shared story and then shared strategy.

## NETWORK VS. PARTNERSHIP

Networks are all the rage, especially in church planting. I think that's because networks allow people to connect with one another around their passion to plant churches while keeping institutional alliances in place, like their denomination. Networks allow multiple relationships at the same time. However, tensions often arise when people who have informally networked together begin to work in partnership.

Chad Clarkson explains that networks usually form around a shared idea or need, and they often stay at the level of idea sharing. Partnerships, on the other hand, are designed to get things done. Typically, partnerships call for high commitment and target specific and measurable results. Networks coordinate information, but partnerships coordinate action.

The Houston Church Planting Network started as a network. Then we developed a partnership with select churches to equip church planters who will plant in the Greater Houston area. To harness the strengths of both a network and partnerships, we keep the network and the partnership separate. HCPN is a network that gathers to encourage church planters, facilitate collaboration and pray informed prayers for the city. But the HCPN Church Planting Residency is a partnership that trains men to become leading church planters in the city.

# CHAPTER 3
## FIVE DYNAMICS OF COLLABORATION

One of my favorite fly-fishing spots is about 10 miles west of Kremmling, Colorado, near the confluence of the Williams Fork and the Colorado River. The giant trees that line the river fill the air with an aroma as sweet as a candy shop. It's shady, and the parking lot is close enough to the water that fishermen are not exhausted by walking to the river in full gear. Best of all, the fishing is great. The fish obviously love this spot too, but not for the same reasons as the fishermen. For the fish, the confluence of two rivers makes the flow powerful. The water boils as two rivers crash together and become one. Each river brings food downstream, so the fish find a shady spot near the confluence and wait for a banquet. Casting my artificial flies amidst the feeding frenzy turns "fishing" into "catching." I love that place.

Establishing the HCPN Church Planting Residency is a confluence of sorts too. Gifts, resources and opportunities have flowed from a dozen churches, crashing together to create something more powerful than any one church could create on its own. Highly gifted church planters have gathered at the confluence to feast on what is coming downstream. It has really been a beautiful thing to see.

As Chad Clarkson and I reflected on how it all came together, we marveled at how much of the residency was beyond our control. And no doubt, we made some mistakes along the way. But I want to revisit some of what we did that we want to keep doing, so that the confluence of resource churches continues to be a beautiful place for potential church planters to get prepared to multiply churches. Here are five things we want to keep doing.

## 1. KEEP SHOWING UP

People collaborate effectively only when they know and trust one another, so we keep showing up to know and love people. In time, trust grows.

Chad is gifted at networking and connecting people to each other. He and I originally met at a conference in another city, and he hung out with our team over meals and between sessions. I was a little surprised that he kept coming around. Since I had just met him, I didn't know if the Amway presentation was coming or if he had his resume in his back pocket or what. But no second shoe dropped. We connected over our common value for church planting. He was just showing up.

I realized later that Chad makes showing up and hanging out with people a way of life. I especially noticed this trait as we began to work together to train church planters. In our meetings, I often heard them talk about how Chad called them and asked them to get together. Potential church planters or pastors would say, "He had no personal agenda. He was not selling anything or trying to get me to do something. He asked straightforward questions about how I see God moving or how he could pray for me. And he listened." Chad was just showing up to see what might happen in the lives of these men.

Chad has noticed that when the Spirit of God is moving in a specific geography, multiple pastors and leaders seem to be hearing the same things. He saw this in Houston. Pastors who did not know one another talked about a growing heart for church planting and collaboration. Because Chad kept showing up in different people's lives, he was able to serve as a connector for pastors. The terms given to people like Chad by experts on collaboration are "alliance champions" and "boundary spanners." This is someone who works in his own network, but at the same time can relate to a larger collaborative network. We have learned that groups don't work together, but people do. When we started HCPN, people from many different groups trusted Chad and showed up too.

Twenty-seven years of serving churches in the same city allowed me to have plenty of opportunities to keep showing up, even though I'm not a gifted networker. I'm actually pretty bad at networking. For years, I kept my head down and planted the church I pastor. In fact, I was among the least likely pastors to show up at a pastors' luncheon. But when I started thinking about how we need to collaborate with other churches, I began to make showing up a priority. The more I showed up, the more relationships of trust were built.

Showing up takes many forms. We showed up by hosting a church-planting conference for Acts 29. We showed up by offering the coaching center for church planters for years. We showed up when other pastors or churches asked us to share with them what we were doing to plant churches. We started the HCPN gathering to give people a good reason to show up. When people get together in the same room to pray together and love the city together and strengthen church planters together, they will eventually begin to work together too.

Looking back, we believe that showing up all those years was foundational to building enough trust among other churches that eventually became willing to collaborate with us to train church planters. Each cup of coffee, lunch, prayer gathering, or coaching conversation created a little more trust with others. And when we asked some to join us in the work of training church planters, they showed up too.

We want to keep showing up. Jeff Wells serves on the residency board of directors. He and I regularly meet with pastors who attend the HCPN gathering or pastors who partner with us in the residency. We sat down with our calendars and scheduled opportunities to show up as much as seemed reasonable. At lunch, we just ask questions and listen to see what God might be doing.

## 2. KEEP IT SIMPLE

People have the best opportunity to collaborate when their common purpose for working together is clear and simple. Because we want to collaborate with churches from different denominations, with some doctrinal differences, and from different ethnicities and geographies, we must keep the end game simple. Simplicity makes it possible to focus on what we want together without getting distracted by our differences.

For example, The HCPN Church Planting Residency is a finishing school for church planters who want to plant and multiply a gospel-centered church in the Greater Houston area. Furthermore, we want candidates who have the potential to lead networks of church planters in the city. This is specific enough to be simple. The specificity makes it easier for people with some differences to know whether they can collaborate. Let me explain.

We are a finishing school. As I noted in chapter 2, we can identify three kinds of church- planting residencies. I want to elaborate a bit on each one:

FOUNDATIONAL RESIDENCY:    Residents learn **general models** for ministry

Education is the primary purpose

2+ years before planting

FUNCTIONAL RESIDENCY:    Residents learn **one church's model** for ministry

Experience is the primary purpose

1-2 years before planting

FINISHING RESIDENCY:    Residents **determine their model** for ministry

Implementation is the primary purpose

12-18 months before planting

We chose to focus on helping church planters finish their preparation, and we invest one year in their preparation. We focus on a particular geography: the Greater Houston area. If someone wants to plant somewhere else, we will celebrate their vision and commitment, but we don't add them to our residency. People who want to participate in a residency that teaches a specific model for ministry soon discover that we are not a fit for them. Our goal isn't to promote one model for ministry; our goal is to help the church planters "determine their model for ministry."

By narrowing our focus, we broaden collaboration. I know that sounds counterintuitive. You would think that the broader the focus, the more likely the collaboration, but the opposite is true. Pastors and churches with many differences can be confident to collaborate if we can agree on the specific shared goals and unifying essential beliefs. In our case, that's the gospel. Church elder boards and missions committees can understand and support our working together if we keep it simple.

## 3. KEEP ON KEEPING ON

Perseverance is the ability to "keep on keeping on." Don't quit. Keep going even if it's hard. Perseverance is the only way we get things done. We already understood the principle, but we were surprised that our perseverance to establish the Houston Church Planting Network impacted others. Our perseverance gave us credibility with others.

Clear Creek Community Church bore the burden of HCPN for four years because we believed it was a great need in our city, and that God was leading us to do it. We learned that our commitment to "do it alone" was part of what compelled people to "do it together." Perseverance built credibility, and credibility fostered collaboration. If you want to create this kind of network, you will probably have to persevere for a season of "doing it alone" so that people see your commitment, and then have confidence to join you and "do it together."

Perseverance includes waiting. We tell church planters, "Nothing grows fast but a weed." In other words, planting a church takes time. It might grow more slowly than you think it should. The same is true of collaboration. It took longer than we initially assumed, but God used the period of waiting to strengthen our convictions about church planting in the city and to strengthen our credibility with other church leaders in the city.

I've been deer hunting one time. My friend, who owned the land where I hunted, placed me in a deer blind and said, "If you wait long enough, you will have the opportunity to get a big deer." He explained, "The does will come first, then the small bucks, then the big bucks." A smile came to his face when he concluded, "That's how they came to be big bucks." It happened just as he said.

I thought about my singular hunting experience as I remembered how participants emerged in HCPN. Don't get me wrong; we were not trying to "bag" anyone, large or small, but aspiring church planters seemed to jump at the chance to collaborate. Yet the longer we waited and persevered, the more we connected with larger churches with available resources for partnership. In retrospect, it makes perfect sense. Larger churches have lots of requests for resources. As good stewards, they look for opportunities with proven track records. When you keep on keeping on, you build credibility with larger churches, and some of them choose to join you in your work.

Today, as we aspire to multiply our work, we're reminded of the power of perseverance. We hope for a groundswell of collaboration to help multiply residencies. We pray for revival in our city so that God might use us to encourage other great cities, but we realize we have no control over these things. By God's grace, we will simply keep on keeping on.

## 4. KEEP SHARING THE MIC

The room was buzzing with the conversations of church planters around the tables at one of the gatherings of the Houston Church Planting Network. A pastor of a resource church approached Chad. While marveling at the spirit of love and cooperation in the room, he told Chad, "One reason this works so well is that you don't want to be king."

Collaboration requires humble leadership. For partnership to grow, leaders must humbly share the leadership, especially the "upfront" leadership. That's why we say, "Keep sharing the mic." Chad and I have some "upfront" opportunities, but most of the time we put the microphone in another leader's hand. Early on, we realized that the more I was up front, the more HCPN would seem like "my thing," which would undermine our desire for collaboration. Also, we rarely meet at a Clear Creek Community Church location, and I hold the mic only once or twice a year. Although Chad is the director, he's rarely up front. Other pastors and leaders host our gatherings, lead us in prayer, and speak at our gatherings of church planters.

Behind the scenes, collaborative works require outstanding leadership and plenty of communication. Chad works with others to develop a strategic plan for HCPN gatherings. We have a board of directors that oversees budgets and determines direction, and, when we gather, we keep sharing the mic.

Sharing the mic allows us to highlight multiple models of ministry, demonstrate our commitment to ethnic diversity, and provide opportunities for emerging leaders to be known, The more that the microphone is in one person's hand, the less likely we are to feel like the work is in all of our hands.

## 5. KEEP INCLUDING OTHERS

Multiplication requires that we keep including others. It's true in the church, and it's true in any collaborative work. If we are not deliberate, however, time will work against us. The longer an organization exists, the more difficult it is for new people to feel included. Longtime members tend to connect with people they know, and the communication is focused on those who are already part of the organization.

We follow two principles to keep including others at HCPN. First, we want to add value to each person's life and ministry. We want them to meet people who will encourage them, we want them to be prayed for and to pray with others for our city, and we want to strengthen them with inspirational training. We intentionally connect people so that they can meet and pray with people they don't know, which provides opportunity for old-timers to connect with newbies. As they share their experiences, people naturally feel connected and included.

Second, we create multiple onramps with varying levels of commitment required. We begin by asking people to give us their email address so that we can keep them informed about future gatherings. We also invite people to join HCPN by listing their church or network among the members of HCPN on the website, Members are invited, but not required, to assist in funding HCPN. Finally, we invite people to partner with us in the HCPN Church Planting Residency. When individuals and churches collaborate to train church planters, the commitments are greater. Anchor churches—the highest level of commitment—give $100,000 per year to fund the residency, and these pastors commit to participate in training residents. Other partners help fund the work with lesser amounts.

We include others by making the expectations clear and asking for commitments. When we celebrate the training of new church planters and the planting of new churches, we know that we did it together.

# EPILOGUE
## IT'S YOUR MOVE

The Houston Church Planting Network and The HCPN Church
Planting Residency feel really big and really small at the same time. God
brought people together from different parts of the city, having different
denominations and ethnicities, and with different theological distinctives
to work together to train church planters to plant churches to reach every
man, woman and child in the city with the gospel.

On one hand, that seems big. But let's be honest. The immediate impact
of this work in light of the overwhelming need is very, very small. Oh,
I know the story of the guy who was saving starfish on the beach, and
I know that this work matters to each church planter and every person
impacted by a church. But seven potential church planters in a city of
more than 6 million people that is growing by 2,300 people per week (the
equivalent of one megachurch) with 220 different language groups has the
impact potential of seven people trying to extinguish a forest fire with spit.
This work is small, unless this work includes the DNA of multiplication.

Multiplication could happen if this work provides a model, coaching
and enough traction to inspire apostolic leaders, network leaders, private
donors and potential church planters to invest their lives in works like this
one. If our collaboration multiplies, we could see scores of collaborative
residencies develop in Houston in a few short years. Each residency will
include a dozen or so churches, thus tapping into more and more latent
Kingdom resources. In turn, there will be new church planters committed
to multiplying churches. It will not happen overnight, but in our lifetime,
we really can see the multiplication of churches and movements covering
Houston like a wildfire claims a windswept prairie.

If that happens in Houston, or in your city, maybe God will ignite hope in the overwhelmed pastors of other world-class cities. And they will take the risks to collaborate too. Maybe they will gather to strengthen church planters, pray for the city and foster collaboration. Maybe they will push through tensions to learn to work together. Maybe their collaboration will also turn to multiplication, and then it will happen again and again.

Multiplying movements need a place to start. I'm hoping that God might use the Houston Church Planting Network and The HCPN Church Planting Residency as places to start a movement for the sake of Houston, Texas, and for the glory of God.

The movement in your city needs a place to start. I hope it starts with you.

# ABOUT THE AUTHOR

Bruce Wesley is the founding pastor of Clear Creek Community Church. Since launching in fall 1993, the church has grown to an average weekly attendance of more than 5,000 people at three campuses. Bruce serves as senior pastor, giving oversight to strategic leadership and spiritual formation, and he serves as one of the primary preachers. He holds an M.Div. from Southwestern Baptist Theological Seminary and a D.Min. from New Orleans Baptist Theological Seminary.

Bruce is the founder, president and executive board member of the Houston Church Planting Network, a network of 30-plus networks working together to strengthen church planters to reach every man, woman and child in Greater Houston. In 2014, HCPN started the HCPN Church Planting Residency, a paid residency program for church planters led by key pastors from across the city.

Bruce serves as an executive board member of Acts 29 Church Planting Network, a diverse global network of church-planting churches.

Bruce and his wife Susan invest in three key areas for community transformation: planting churches, strengthening marriages and raising up leaders for the church of tomorrow. He loves the mountains, fly fishing and hiking trails.

# RESOURCES

## THE INTENTIONAL LEADER SERIES

The Intentional Leader Series is brought to you by the Auxano Team. We invite you to check out the suite of resources at VisionRoom.com, including:

Practical solutions for church leaders
through book summaries

High-level thinking.
Ground-level application.

---

# auxano®

auxano.com | visionroom.com | willmancini.com

Other books in the Intentional Leader Series:

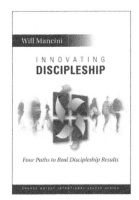
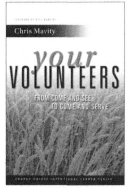
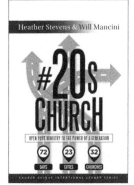

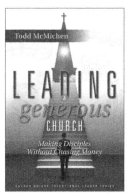

Upcoming Books in the Intentional Leader Series:

**Less Church, More Life:**
**Why Churches Do Too Much and What To Do About It**
by Will Mancini

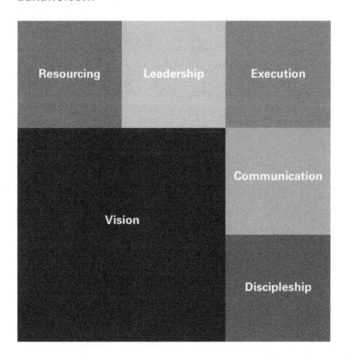

# ≡XPONENTIAL⌐
## RESOURCING CHURCH PLANTERS

- Largest annual gatherings of church planters in the world (Florida & Southern CA)

- 75+ FREE eBooks

- 400+ Hours of FREE Audio Training via podcasts from national leaders

- 30+ Hours of Video Training from national leaders

- FREE weekly email newsletter

- Missional and Discipleship Learning Communities

- Church Planters Blog

- Conference content available via Digital Access Pass

## exponential.org >

@churchplanting
info@exponential.org

BRUCE WESLEY